T0078107

NAVIGATING THE GRAY

Asha Bianca

WESTBOW
PRESS®
A DIVISION OF THOMAS NELSON
& ZONDERVAN

Scriptures taken from the Holy Bible, New International Version®, NIV®. Copyright © 1973, 1978, 1984, 2011 by Biblica, Inc.™ Used by permission of Zondervan. All rights reserved worldwide. www.zondervan.com The "NIV" and "New International Version" are trademarks registered in the United States Patent and Trademark Office by Biblica, Inc

WestBow Press books may be ordered through booksellers or by contacting:

WestBow Press
A Division of Thomas Nelson & Zondervan
1663 Liberty Drive
Bloomington, IN 47403
www.westbowpress.com
1 (866) 928-1240

ISBN: 978-1-9736-1245-2 (sc)
ISBN: 978-1-9736-1244-5 (e)

Print information available on the last page.

WestBow Press rev. date: 01/04/2018

Loving those you disagree with and working well together.

CONTENTS

WELCOME

Thank you for choosing this book and welcome to a dialogue about loving individuals who we don't agree with and leading well at work. First, I am certain there are perspectives that I have written that you will disagree with so thank you in advance for already practicing loving without fully agreeing.

We are on this journey together and please know that I already want to hear about your story, all the Ins & outs, upside downs. You have my ear and now my book. Thank you for living your life boldly and know I welcome you into my story as well.

I write from my heart and the place that I am at in my own experiences and beliefs. I appreciate you, and look forward to gaining your perspective as well as answering any additional questions you may have via email at ashabianca@gmail.com.

INTRODUCTION

"We need not think alike to love alike."
—Francis David

Sometimes we just disagree. The source of our stance can be our own experiences, upbringing, passions or wiring but simply put, each of us is different. Learning how to love the differences and not make them feel threatening or forced on us is the point of this book.

For some reason, there is this fear that if I listen to someone who shares something I disagree with that I am somehow compromising my stance. This is the primary thought I'd like to challenge in this book. I want to explore how to have authentic hard conversations or sometimes silence, depending on the topic and approach with those we love. We will cover how to navigate the areas of conflict with someone that don't align with our beliefs.

The title itself is the summary of this book. Most of us are familiar with black and white scenarios. It is the gray that itself lends to an unfamiliarity and opportunity to deepen our relationships. Let's say I agree with 100% of my entire circle, this is fairly black and white. First, this is make believe because we know no one is exactly the same. If this were true though, there would be nothing for us to navigate through. If we were always in agreement, how could our relationship deepen. What is more likely is that we have figured out which topics to avoid because we don't know yet how to navigate the gray areas in our relationship. Living authentically, truly respecting each other is found in navigating the gray areas with those we truly invest in.

For the most part, we speak very little about our heart issues. For all that technology has done to connect the world, our heart talks and authentic relationships have been reduced instead of deepened. Individuals feel more isolated today than they did before they could log-on and be instantly "connected" to the world. Whether you walk down the street in a small town where everyone knows your name or in a large city with the masses, few know your heart, woes, and what keeps you up late at night. I'm not sure why this is but I set off to explore it in this book.

There are hopefully a few individuals in your circle who you have allowed to talk deeply with about some of the most controversial topics in your life. These individuals have earned that right through relationship. They have been safe, trusted confidantes with some of the most delicate parts of yourself. They have listened without judgement, they have focused on being there for you. This presence has been the priority, more than agreeing with you.

Part one is focused on navigating the gray in your life at home. However, the large majority of us work outside the home as well, so I've included a part two. Part two focuses on how to lead your life well in a work environment. I firmly believe that you are the leader of your own life, actions, words, decisions, behaviors and attitude.

Similarly to how you can tell a team to trust or respect you and it doesn't just happen. Love and relationships whether at home or work don't just happen either. The focus of this book is learning how to love well even when we disagree and work well even in tough circumstances.

Let's roll-up our sleeves, and most importantly perk up our ears and hearts.

PART
1

LOVING THOSE WE DISAGREE WITH, NAVIGATING THE GRAY AT HOME

EVERY PERSON HAS A STORY

A person's a person no matter how small.

– Dr. Seuss

I love this quote, mostly because it resonates with my faith that I am valued. That every single individual on this earth is valued enough to die for and yes, enough to love. Think about this for a minute, every person has a story and that story, even if we think is small, to God and to that person is big. We can't walk in their shoes, see what they've seen and so who are we to even call a story or a person small, or less than.

For a moment, truly challenge yourself, do you believe this statement that every person has a story? If you did it might look like this. I have no idea of the ways this person thinks, works, rationalizes, gets engaged, listens, talks and in order to really know them, I may need to invest more than 10 seconds before I think I know just what they should do as they cut me off in traffic. Or it could look like this perhaps my grumpy family member had a time when they were in the middle of a different season that I don't even know about, perhaps I need to pause on my quick judgements about what they know and instead just listen, to their story.

Yes, its that practical. Regardless of whether we are talking about those closest to us or those who we bump into on the street, every single person has a story. Part of the human experience is in saying, I don't know what you're going through. I really have no idea what that might be like but I want to be with you through it. There is something powerful and beautiful about this statement. The effort of understanding, truly taking the time to understand, is something our fast paced, instant gratification culture is becoming too busy for. The problem with us not spending the time to know and understand individuals who we love is that we can't love them real or well.

Recently, I learned that someone close to me is afraid to swim. This finding was foreign to me. Let me explain part of my story and why this wasn't a natural thought for me. The ocean was a part of my childhood in a way that a grandma or grandpa might be for others. We went there and played for hours. If we weren't at the ocean, we were hanging at some friend's pool to get our swimming time in. There were many reasons for this, I grew up in Southern California, without much money. The beach was free. It allowed for hours and hours of free entertainment. The ocean and water in general is a key part of who I am.

When I became a mom, it was critical to teach my daughter to swim, I had her at the beach and in the pool swimming without floating devices before she was one year old. This was because I wanted it to be a part of her world, not one where she would ever fear or be uncomfortable in. This was part of my heart's desire but is also a very real practical safety provision. Most people in Southern California have access to water, our condo had a pool and I realized that she would be near water at an early age. Part of my making sure she was equipped and had survival skills in her environment was to teach her to swim.

My friend who is afraid of the water, is 62 years old and grew-up in farm country, Wisconsin. Her experiences with water started much later in life, by the time she had her first water experiences, she already had a self-consciousness that others were ahead in the swimming game, which then led to her not being comfortable and scary situations being the result. The pay-off to learn was too high, as the possibilities were most probably injury or embarrassment. Neither of these possibilities were worth the risk to learn. Not to mention, the only water opportunities were far and few in-between.

So I take these couple paragraphs to say that when my friend tells me she is afraid of the water. I have a choice to make. I can either come from my experience which is screaming, what in the world, how could you be afraid of the water? why have you not learned in all these years? how can you miss out on the incredible experience that water is?" or I can lean in, I can inquire, be sensitive to a difference and invest in the relationship by recognizing we are in a gray area here where I don't know where this individual is coming from and why. The issue isn't a black and white one to her like it was for me. How I made her feel about sharing this information was more important than her understanding my perspective. We were relatively new friends, knowing one another for less than a year. In relationship terms, this is a very short time.

I use this example, which is fairly light hearted in nature to start us down this road of understanding, every person has a story. Some of the topics we dive into are going to be much more challenging to navigate, for instance atheism, divorce, homosexuality, and addictions. Loving an individual and meeting them in the gray is extremely challenging and requires the spirit's leading, particularly in these areas.

Storytelling is one of my favorite ways to learn, it is one of the reasons Jesus was such a good teacher. Jesus knew that if he could explain the truth in the form of a story, not only would it resonate deep in the human heart but it was portable. When communication relied heavily on travelers on foot the message needed to be memorable.

3

Stories are memorable, especially when they speak directly to where we are at a time of need, joy, sorrow, and in the face of a tragedy.

The thing with storytelling is it takes two, the person telling the story and the person receiving the story. Listening is just as active as talking in true story telling. Understanding, truly understanding where someone comes from and why they may do what they do is part of loving the real someone.

Also, a point needs to be made that I can completely disagree with someone and still give the relationship, the respect to listen to them. Important enough to say again, I can listen, attempt to understand their story and still completely disagree with them, while loving them still. Somehow we have associated listening to each other as automatic agreement or if we know someone will most likely not agree with our choices or part of the story, we self-audit and choose a different group to share those pieces with.

This is an inauthenticity that gets in the way of real relationships. The gift of authentic real loving relationships is that nothing you can say about your opinions, unless it's directly abusive to me, should I feel unsafe about hearing. For those who we are pouring into, and who pour into us, trust needs to supersede judging and love needs to be the goal.

The story of the woman caught in the act of adultery and drug to Jesus in the courtyard to be tried comes immediately to mind. Here was a woman caught in an act that law said she could be stoned for. Jesus instantly recognized the condemnation and shame that she felt. He knelt to her and called her daughter. That in itself is such a huge visual of the way He met her where she was. I love what He told the crowd of accusers, "Let he without sin, cast the first stone" (John 8:7). Now Jesus, didn't agree with adultery but He was too busy with her heart and story and the realness that every single one of us fall short to do anything but love her. He didn't choose this moment to start preaching the problems that adultery causes, how she is seeking love outside of Him, how the crowd was right, how it would be legal to stone her, He focused on her. He met her where she was, protected her by equalizing the truth that each of us have a story, a struggle, moments where we are imperfect. He navigated the gray, He loved instead of judged, He taught the individuals in the moment how to love first, He won the day, which in this case was her heart. He also did it in an uncompromising way to the truth He knew, he didn't say adultery was ok, he didn't muddy the black and whiteness of the issue. Instead He met her and loved her well.

This is the Jesus who I yearn to become. When I see a situation, I so want to size it up in 30 seconds. Oh, this was what he or she was doing and why. It's my natural tendency to judge when I don't understand. This is when I have to remember the helping spirit who can help me focus on loving. Sometimes the right call is to be silent, sometimes its to inquire, sometimes its to help, sometimes its to pray out-loud, sometimes it to pray to myself. There are many ways the spirit may lead you in a situation that seems black and white but is clearly gray in this world, while our view is partial.

As we step into topics that challenge us to look outside our own perspective, I wanted to start with this chapter because until we truly see the hearts of others and them through our mighty God's eyes, it will be challenging to open our ears or our hearts to their experiences or opinions.

By acknowledging that each person has their own story, we can move on to how to engage with that story.

Now, it is equally important to state that while every person has a story, it doesn't mean you have to be in it. If they have been abusive, harmful, or taken advantage of you, theirs may be a story that you create some boundaries around. It may even take redefining who they are to you. Loving an individual who is abusive, addicted, harmful to themselves and others can be not engaging in their story.

I do think we are quick to judge many times based on the type of issues a person deals with. Its helpful to remember that sin is not graded on a bell curve, there isn't one that is worse than others. I write from my heart and that means I have to share about God's work in my life. From my experience, he is my all in all. I love this verse because it talks about the new creation that I am, 2 Corinthians 5:17, "Therefore, if anyone is in Christ, he is a new creation. The old has passed away; behold, the new has come."

As a Christian, I've had several eye opening moments. One of them was when I learned that every sin, regardless of whether its gossip or murder is still sin. Sure there are different degrees of consequences to sin here on earth but to God's heart, we all fall short and there isn't one sin that is more acceptable than another sin to Him. He loves us anyway! Despite the struggles, despite our will, our want to and heart is what he longs for. He longs for relationship with us. At the heart of every issue is our ability to find the love that supports the relationship and lean in to it with authenticity.

One of the most hypocritical parts of our world is thinking that one sin is more acceptable than another. When we see all sin as sin, it allows us to understand the need for love first in all situations. So I haven't struggled in my own life with drunkenness. It's not an area that I have a lot of experience with. However, I have struggled with pride. For me to look on a brother and sister of Christ who is struggling with an alcohol addiction and judge them would be hypocritical since I know that every single one of us struggle with something.

I thank God for this, that we all fall short and that there is no condemnation. This is the most freeing part for relationships. Since God is the judge and the jury, there is no reason that I should pretend I am. My job on earth is to love people, pure and simple, He orchestrates the rest. I don't have to carry the load of making people see the error of their ways. I can be real and honest about my own challenges so there is a comfortable and safe place for them to be real but I don't need to be hyper-concerned with how I'm going to change them because honestly, I'm not. God may as they let Him, He may use me to help them see Him in a new way. If that happens; it is a blessing. That can't be where I start though. I need to start by saying ok, here is a person who has a story, who has a struggle and who I get the chance to bless or love today. The rest is God's job.

There is a phrase that is quite visual in the Bible, it is to "cast one's burdens," (Psalm 55:22). This visual is so helpful for me because it is actually taking the weight that I feel about areas I am not sure how to navigate and giving them to God so I can be light enough to move easily in His will. I think of Mohammad Ali, he prided himself on being fast on his feet and beating individuals by moving around in a very light manner. He wasn't held down by his past, by the struggle that he experienced, he overcame that weight and instead did what he did best. He was able to because he knew who he was and what he needed to do in the ring. This visual of being light on my feet by not being burdened by my own judgement of someone else is one I encourage you to hold fast to during the next more challenging chapters.

Some of us hang on to struggles more tightly than others. For instance if our own child is struggling with their sexuality or an addiction, we may feel less inclined to cast that burden to God, where it truly belongs. Then, we aren't free to love them the way we need to because we are carrying their burden instead of relying on God to do His job. When our children get older, somehow we think that boundaries don't apply, and they are still our children when in reality they were on loan to us the entire time, they are God's.

There is a saying to treat your friends like family and your family like friends. I really like this idea because I think we sometimes get too comfortable with family members and it implies a tendency that may become disrespectful. Also, I think sometimes we don't let friends get close enough to see the junk in our lives and this stalls the relationship from deepening. By allowing friends to see parts of you that family may only see, it opens up your authenticity to another group of individuals who can speak into your circumstance. By placing a bit more manners and formality between your relationship with your family, it can help root it in respect as opposed to a disrespectful comfort.

To close out this chapter and move on to the meat of our most controversial topics, I found a verse that I absolutely love. This verse at its heart is about being a peacemaker. Matthew 5:9 reads: "Blessed are the peacemakers, for they will be called children of God." You're blessed when you can show people how to cooperate instead of compete or fight. That's when you discover who you really are, and your place in God's family.

What a gift to be able to navigate the gray as a peacemaker, a gift for you and from you. To cooperate instead of compete or fight, to listen to a story and know a name.

> "If your name isn't known, then it's a very lonely feeling."
>
> - Madeleine L'Engle

Yes, this quote hits me and almost makes me teary, to know and be known without judgment is to be loved….Onward!

Tips to remember when valuing people where they are:

1) They may be doing the very best they possibly can be. Sometimes we put expectations on others that are frankly

unrealistic for where they are in their current journey. Error on the side of generous grace with expectations.

2) Listen, truly listen. If you are in a rush or not able to fully listen, please let them know that they are important to you and you'd like to pick up on this important conversation at another time when you both can be present and listen fully. Please don't half listen, especially when someone is pouring out their story and heart. Its better to be authentic with where you are at in the moment as opposed to going through the motions and them feeling unheard.

3) Make an effort to treat strangers kindly. One of the benefits of living in a small town right now is there is a good likelihood that I know the individuals somehow in my town, through a sister/brother or friend. It helps remind me that every one is someone's daughter/son/brother/mom. It costs nothing to be kind and can be the very encouragement that makes a difference in another's life.

Q & A about Every Person has a Story:

Q: What if I have heard a person's story over and over and they just seem stuck in it?

A: This can be tricky because you may be expecting them to "get over" something in the time you would take to. Part of each person having their story means, they are free to hold on to what they want to when they want to. I think a practical response to this is to be there for them in listening without trying to "fix" them. If you truly can't listen to this story one more time, whether it is about their abuse, mean boss, disrespectful kids, I think the best next step is to pray for them. Even if it is while you are listening to their story on auto-repeat, pray that they would have freedom from this particular burden. This is the most powerful way that I have seen change. Sometimes our presence, silence and prayer is the best gift of friendship that we can give.

Q: My adult children expect me to be a part of every decision and problem on their plate, how do I create some space between their story and mine?

A: Tough situation when adult children still expect you to parent them full-time. This relationship is meant to evolve and can be healthy without proper guiding. I find that being really clear with what you believe your role should be in the situation helps with questions such as, are you a listener? Is there a part of this problem that you've contributed to? Have you owned up to that part? Showing empathy then redirected ownership as you would for a friend also helps, with phrases such as,"That must be really frustrating, what are you thinking you'll do?" By remembering that they have their own story, that you get to be a part of, but that is theirs it will help you not take on another story when you have your own to live.

Q: I just don't want to hear their story, I disagree with it so strongly that I can't even stand to hear it, how do I have any relationship with them?

A: If you're unable to get past your own opinion and listen to what their story really is, it's going to be challenging to have an authentic relationship. You may have to avoid each other, or talk about the weather, sports or some other filler for the rest of your life. This may be just fine if this isn't a person who you have on your heart to have a deep relationship with. However, if you do long for a deeper relationship, chances are you are going to hear things that may trigger you and you'll want to pray for a spirit of openness and no offense to ensure you are listening well.

Q: How can I listen to their story when they've hurt me so badly and deny that they did?

A: This may be a relationship that you don't pursue if it has caused you great pain and there is a likelihood that you may experience great pain again because they haven't spent the time and energy to come to terms with their actions or words. In some cases, not being part of their story is actually a way to love them and protect yourself. The most practical way to love them is through prayer, it is safe and powerful for you. God is a powerful redeemer who can heal the deepest hurts. This doesn't mean however that we need to subject ourselves to individuals who don't own the part of their story that has been harmful to others.

WHAT DOES LOVE LOOK LIKE?

Love is patient, love is kind. It does not envy, it does not boast, it is not proud. It does not dishonor others, it is not self-seeking, it is not easily angered, it keeps no record of wrongs.
– 1 Corinthians 13:4-5

First, I need to be completely honest with you, I love the word love. Everything about it makes me smile. I am a fan of hearts. My dad used to give me heart stickers in fact to share with my classroom on the first day of school. I am a fan of love in every healthy way possible. That said, I have tried very hard during this chapter to keep my zeal for love a part from my mental awareness of what it actually is. A more cerebral truth vs feelings based understanding of what it is. As part of this process, I purposefully chose the word "look" instead of "feel" for this chapter. I think the feelings of our world have really mixed up the truth of what love actually looks like.

Love to me looks like a safe place where I know someone has me in their heart and will not cause me to stumble in anyway because they love me that much. It is patience at its core that when I was little, learning to walk, love didn't yell at me to hurry up and just get it done. Instead love waited, supported, cheered and was that whisper saying try again honey. Love celebrated every step before it came to be with a patient hope. Love didn't have an expectation or timeline or agenda.

Love is not harsh words. Love is not mean. Love is kind. The word kind defined as, "Helpful, considerate, thoughtful, good". Love is all of these things. Love thinks before it speaks, listens before reacting and puts aside its own preference for a genuine authentic exchange rooted in relationship.

Love does not think that by listening to someone else's opinion, mine is devalued. Love doesn't envy time, attention or words that way. Love doesn't try to steal the "right" status in an effort to feel unhealthy pride. My way or the highway doesn't exist in conversations with love. Love does not act on pretense or expectations, love clarifies it engages. It asks open ended questions without having a pre-planned answer.

Love does not dishonor others. This one bears repeating in our world today, Love does not dishonor others. Wait a minute, who is others? Just people who agree with me? No, others is every other person in this world. Love does not dishonor others, period. If you're dishonoring others, even if you couldn't disagree with them more, you are not loving them. As a Christian, we are called to Love God and Love Others. This is a commandment not a suggestion. There is a key reason for it. When we pridefully pretend like we know everything and start projecting dishonor on others, our words and actions of hate are speaking so loudly that our God's action of love is forgotten. The very effort that we want to do, be glory bearers and light carriers for God is dulled, dimmed and hidden by our agendas being in the way. Love is not self-seeking. Love doesn't wish to lift ourselves up. When we truly love well, our spirits are definitely encouraged but that isn't the reason we love, it is a byproduct of loving well.

Love is not easily angered, let's hover here for a minute. One of the best, fairly common examples I have observed of this is regularly a group of people I know would attend a church service and then eat out. During the restaurant experience, something would happen. The waitress would forget something, the food would be wrong, the tone of the hostess's voice wasn't welcoming, the people in the next booth were being rude….Oh my goodness! Ok, if you are trying to be loving, please have a long fuse. If you can't have a long fuse, stay away from people until you can. Easily angered is one of the key tells that you are not being loving. Easily offended by what that mother in law says, or your spouse, stop in your tracks and believe the best about them. Now some people are trying to be mean, call that bologna out but try to operate your days as if in general, people aren't trying to anger or offend you. Try to keep yourself in check when it comes to the little things in life and as your perspective and love grows you'll notice that pretty soon your able to not be easily angered by big things as well. You can make changes in your life to ensure the big offenses and justifiable anger is addressed but you actually have a choice to get angry about them. Most times this anger is not helpful to the cause or to loving well. It genuinely results in a backlash that is misunderstood and causes more harm than good.

Love is a bit like a dog in that it doesn't remember how long you've been gone for the day or when you yelled at it, it loves you regardless. It keeps no record of wrongs, it has a short memory. Now if a dog is being beaten, dangerously neglected, or abused, it should find a new owner but for the most part it carries on without any baggage of the negative remember whens. We can learn a lot about love from a dog in this sense. Forgetting past pain frees us to love bigger and more freely. By addressing the pain in the moment, seeking healing and moving on, we can close that chapter and guess what we never have to open it again! God may find it helpful for you to on special occasion share that particular chapter with someone in a similar place but it will be a different angle of sharing. Once we are healed from a past wrong, we can share it without it stealing our joy. We can share it to inspire a new chapter being possible.

Love looks like a safe place to be together in truth and authenticity. This also means that you don't have to gloss over what you disagree with, sometimes you won't need to say a word and sometimes you'll ask for a gentle way to share your heart. Love values the relationship above all, it doesn't mean you compromise what you believe it means you can stand on your truth without standing on another person.

I will tell you I don't think I could have described as clearly what love was even five short years ago. I was in a fog of what love was supposed to be too heavy to know what love really looks like. I can tell you now that love is sometimes the word done, stop, no. Love is not pretending it is an authentic exchange that allows light to shine on truth as opposed to be hidden in the darkness.

What makes you vulnerable, makes you beautiful. There's a word for it. Authentic. - Tim Brown

This quote is freeing for me because what made me vulnerable was my misunderstanding of what love looked like in the past. Now I can allow that beauty to shine truth into what love looks like today. Love means that even if I have a moment or many of being unloving, I have a safe place to lean in and know that I have grace in that moment. I am not perfect, I am perfectly loved and through that I can, with the spirit's leading, love well.

My coworker shared this with me, it summarized my thoughts on love as it relates to relationships pretty well: Marriage is not what everyone thinks it is. It's not waking up early every morning to make breakfast and eat together. It's not cuddling in bed together until both of you peacefully fall asleep. It's not a clean home and a homemade meal every day. It's someone who steals the covers and elbows you in the face. It's a few harsh words, fights and the silent treatment, it's wondering if you've made the right decision. It is, despite all of those things, the one thing you look forward to every day. It's coming home to the same person everyday that you know loves and cares about you. It's laughing about the one time you accidentally did something stupid. It's about eating the cheapest and easiest meal you can make and sitting down together at 10pm to eat because you both had a crazy day. It's when you have an emotional breakdown and they hold you and tell you everything is going to be okay, and you believe them. It's about still loving someone even though they make you absolutely insane. Living with the person you love is fights about absolutely nothing, but is also having a love that people spend their whole life looking for. It's not perfect and it's hard, but it's amazing and comforting and the best thing you'll ever experience. But more importantly, it is never, EVER giving up on each other, no matter what.

This quote summarizes my thoughts on being a parent the best that I've found to date:

> Making the decision to have a child — it is momentous.
> It is to decide forever to have your heart go walking
> around outside your body.
> – Elizabeth Stone

This quote summarizes my thoughts on loving all others, especially well:

> "You can kiss your family and friends good-bye and
> put miles between you, but at the same time you
> carry them with you in your heart, your mind, your
> stomach, because you do not just live in a world but a
> world lives in you."
> – Frederick Buccaneer

A couple tips for What Love Looks Like:

1) Actions speak way louder than words when it comes to what love looks like. If you are being told one thing but treated very differently this is not love.

2) You can love someone as a child of God without wanting them in your story. Some people have lost the right to be in your story any longer and that is ok. However, they still deserve to be treated with respect and you love them without allowing them to harm you.

3) Keep level headed. If you are dating someone make sure not to have sex with them, it will fog your thinking and all of a sudden feelings will take over. The part of you that can discern what love looks like will be clouded and your judgement may be impaired. This is my belief because of what I've seen sex outside of marriage do to individuals, particularly individuals who already have children. All of a sudden, their children are no longer their priority and they are losing their mind, so to speak because they fell so in love. This is lust not love, know the difference.

Q & A for What Love Looks Like:

Q: People toss around the word love without it meaning anything, doesn't this bother you?

A: I do have some close friends who this really bothers. For me, it's not an issue at all. I have been a youth leader for a long time and I'll tell you teens say I love you more than even toddlers I think. However, you know I think there are a lot worse things people could be saying to each other.

Q: If I love my boyfriend, truly love him, why can't I make love to him?

A: Well this is the beauty of free will, you actually can. That wouldn't be my choice, in fact it hasn't been for the last two years that I've been dating someone. Not because I don't want to because I truly believe what science and more importantly the bible say about the long-term effects of casual sex. There is nothing casual about it. I think it will take a toll on you if you do, cloud your judgement and I also think if he loves you and says he has the same beliefs for you, he'll honor your body until he puts a ring (really two) on it.

Q: I love my same sex partner and have been with them for over a decade, my parent still doesn't understand it?

A: This is a tough one, particularly because you want everyone to love this person as much as you do. However, this is where you'll need to exercise a bit of tolerance with letting this parent be where they are at in their beliefs. For some individuals it's really challenging and completely against the way they have ever known and they may never understand. You have your own story to tell and others may not agree with your story. This is a hard place to be if they are unloving in it. If they can love you while disagreeing, this is the best I'd hope for with casting expectations on someone else.

DON'T MENTION IT

I'm not concerned with your liking or disliking me... All I ask is that you respect me as a human being.

– Jackie Robinson

One of the top issues with how to navigate the gray is actually in the approach. Knowing when and how to say something that is bothering you is absolutely critical. Broaching a sensitive topic well takes thought and planning. One of the things I did poorly as a new mother was have big conversations in the car making short trips in town. So take a lesson from my fail book and remember to allow time for topics that take time. Don't rush the process. Also, recognize that you may be ready to talk about something and the other individual may not be. They actually may never be and that's ok. Assuming we are talking about adults, whether family or not, each individual gets to engage in the conversation willingly. Pressured conversation is ineffective relationship building conversation. So let's say you have an individual in your life, friend, parent, adult child, etc., and you disagree with something you believe is going on in their life that could be harmful. That's the scenario we'll start with. It could be many different reasons why you don't believe this is a positive thing in their life, you have different beliefs, you are observing behaviors in line with negative results, etc.

Our natural tendency in this situation is to either pout or blow-up. Neither of these two options is the most productive. Pouting is where we agree not to mention it and there is a big elephant in the room or our hearts with this person. We haven't really addressed it or let go of it, we're just pretending to be in relationship while pouting. The other equally problematic action is we blow-up, we wait until that one offense occurs, or big occasion and we let it all out, loud and full of self-serving release.

So I would encourage us to take a different path with these situations. First, pray about them, really contemplate what is going on in the circumstance and how important it is for you to address what's bugging you. Give this some time, unless its urgent such-as suicide tendencies, addiction, serious abuse, etc., which are more black and white issues with responses. The gray areas can have a bit of time to pray and ponder approach. Once you feel led to either truly give the concern to God and not address it without pouting or to honorably seek to communicate about it, make sure you feel peace with the direction.

If you chose to not address it directly with the person, make sure you give it to God every single time it comes-up. Don't hold on to it, let it fully free to never burden you again.

If you do chose to address it, give the individual the respect of preparing, no one likes to be surprised especially with sensitive topics. Ask for permission to share something that you have had on your heart, in person ideally. Only if you live nations away from each other, should you be having very hard conversations over the phone, never over text. If you value this relationship, value it enough to give it your time and presence. You'll be able to read the receiver's response exceedingly better if the meeting is in person. If this is an area that you have tried to talk about with them in the past, acknowledge if you have not come with an open heart and open ears. Ask for the chance to talk about it again. Depending on the outcome that you are trying to achieve, you'll want to plan accordingly:

1) Just get something off your chest. Make sure this is really all you want because if there is no change on the receiver's end, will you be disappointed?

   1a) If this is truly what you want to do, then share openly and kindly about something of concern to you. I had to have this type of conversation once with my loved one. I just really wanted her to know what was on my mind about a particular topic. I laid the groundwork that she probably wasn't going to like my opinion but I needed to get it out and appreciated her being open to hear it. I promised her, and kept this promise, that I wouldn't bring it up again since it is her life and story after all.

2) Desiring some change. If the purpose of your conversation is to ask for change, make sure that the change is something within this individual's control, even if they wanted to make it. For instance, don't ask one person about a change of behavior that their spouse does that really rubs you wrong. Directly to the source is the most efficient and respectful way to have this conversation. Anything else feels like gossip and can be very damaging to all relationships involved.

   2a) Recognize that you have no control over an individual other than yourself to change. There are significant consequences to damaging behaviors that you can control but you cannot make someone else change, ever. So if you are desiring someone else to change start with sharing about your own feelings with statements such as I feel hurt when you forget my birthday, would you try and remember it more frequently? This is a subtle issue but a good example of something that someone else could do that would impact you. Owning your feelings is critical in this and clarifying what your expectations are for instance, even if you don't have the funds to buy me a card just calling me and saying happy birthday would bless me hugely. Now make sure what you are asking for would really be ok with you, there are no victims in this conversation. Own the expectations and clarifying them. It's ok to talk about the strain on the relationship caused by occurrences and ask what you can do to help strengthen the relationship.

Recognize that everyone has a different degree of investment in a relationship. It may not be worth the receiver's time and effort to change, they may not have the want to. This is their life and their story, that is their call and will dictate what role they have in your story. You get to choose what role they have in your life.

There is one additional part that fits into this chapter and it has to do with when people who you know seek out your counsel, and they know you don't agree with them. This is an interesting conversation and sometimes falls into the Don't Mention It category. This quote speaks well to it:

> When we ask for advice, we are usually looking for
> an accomplice.
> – Saul Bellow

Keep in mind for those who are asking for your advice, may be looking for you to agree with them. If you value the relationship and know that you can't agree with what they are asking, it may be worth keeping quiet on the topic. It's ok to say, friend I love you but you know I can't say I agree with that when I don't, you sure you want me to weigh in? You may not particularly like what I have to say? Loving others does not mean lying about who you are and what you believe, that is inauthentic. Inauthenticity erodes instead of builds relationship.

I want you to know how important your voice is in your relationships though, you have the power to encourage, edify and speak life into a friend or family members life. Praying and knowing how to speak life is the key. There are opportunities all around for individuals who are looking for input to ensure they don't hurt themselves or act unwisely. It does take time and investment to ensure you are being loving in your approach. Make sure you are committed to the time, and being led by the spirit to be a safe place for them.

I'm sure you don't have much time, but heroes are hard to find Would you be mine? Could you be mine? - Mark Robertson, "Every Word You Said"

Q AND A FOR DON'T MENTION IT:

Q: My family member is addicted to drugs, the rest of our family ignores it, I can't stand to? How do I approach this lovingly?

A: Such a challenging situation, first and foremost know that you are not alone in this, God is with you and seek Him first for direction and comfort. Addiction is a heavy topic because it steals the very person who you love by turning them into someone else. Honesty and stopping any enabling patterns is the first step. Telling them you love them and you won't ignore what they are doing to themselves and their family is key. Providing support that is healthy is also key whether intervention, rehab, counseling, being an ear to listen, these can all be healthy ways to help. Addicts in general can be extremely self-absorbed so its key that you create boundaries to protect yourself as needed. The last thing you want to do is sacrifice your own good in the name of loving someone. Truly loving them is being real with how their actions impact you.

Q: My Ex allows our kids to watch, play and do things that I just flat out don't agree with, how can I influence this?

A: I'm guessing you couldn't influence this while you were married either because we can't change any other person. Although I have empathy for this situation, the gray here is really under their control while your children are with them. Children are very smart though so you modeling healthy practices and having honest adult conversations with your Ex about your preference while respecting their rights will help. Prayer is the way I have found best to deal with this particular one. My hurt and past experiences make it very challenging for me to see clearly, particularly when it comes to my kids, so I definitely need the spirits leading when it comes to showing love in these very challenging circumstances. As your child gets older, they will observe how what you do, say and watch affects the quality of your life versus other choices. Also, if the direction of your Ex puts your child in danger, obviously take the proper next steps but when it comes to the grays of raising kids, prayer and being a role model is powerful.

Q: My family member is living in a way I disagree with and I don't know how to communicate with them?

A: Anytime a family member has a choice that is different from you believe or yours would be, I'd encourage you to take extra care in where your heart is before you communicate. Ensuring that you communicate your truth in a loving way is critically important. I've had individuals say some really hurtful things to me because they didn't understand how I could be divorced and I have felt their judgement. It's a hard place to have an authentic relationship. If it is causing you frustration, definitely pray about it and then remember that this is their story not yours. If they allow you the opportunity to speak into their life, awesome be loving and speak in truth. Know that this is a gift that they have asked you for relationship when it may have been easier not to because of how different you each are. Also, know that just because you listen to an individual doesn't mean you agree with them. You can also be supportive to them without agreeing. I remember a dear friend of mine was telling me about how she was engaging in a level of intimacy with her boyfriend that wasn't my belief, I shared with my friend that I love her but I don't agree with that, I also am not judging her in it. She was being very bold and open and I had that type of relationship where I could share my beliefs and she knew it wasn't an attack on hers. The relationship was strengthened instead of bruised because she was able to be open and I didn't compromise but still loved. It takes thoughtfulness and leading by the spirit but definitely is possible to dialogue about the most challenging topics that exist in our world today.

FAITH

Faith is the strength by which a shattered world shall emerge into the light.

– Helen Keller

I came to be strong in my faith very early in age. I would walk around saying, "White light" as if I could see something that others couldn't. I felt God's hand protecting me at every turn as I was growing up and grew in my faith on my own. I wasn't raised in a religious house and I never went to church. I found church when I was in my mid teens and through the persistent wisdom of a dear pastor and the tugging of the holy spirit, learned how to have faith in something larger than myself. This is the place I write from, please have grace towards me if you have a very different experience. My point is to share my perspective and not devalue yours by any means.

When I asked for hot topics that cause strife in relationships, this one was right on top time and time again. It is interesting to me that what I call my faith, others call religion, some call the universe causes so much strife. It's definitely unnecessary, particularly with the ability to respect others views. We all are different and what I believe and stand firm on shouldn't cast a shadow on what you believe and stand firm on.

Why is it so challenging to share our faith without ruffling others feathers? I think the answer is from centuries and centuries of persecution, forced practices and a human view of religion as opposed to God's view of relationship. If I am sharing and my dear friend says that she believes in the universe not the God I pray to, this doesn't cause me any strife. This is her belief. I believe differently, it doesn't mean I don't love her. I am very passionate about my faith, I am glad to share it with any one who asks why I seem to have a joy regardless of my circumstances but this doesn't make me upset if someone believes differently. It is not my job to convince others of the power of God in their story. I only know my story and that I rely on God every minute of every single day.

Here are a couple tips for how to not force your beliefs on others and to be respectful of how you share about your faith:

1) Don't apologize for what you believe or shy away from sharing. If you believe a certain way, it is ok to share. If an individual doesn't agree with you, guess what, that is ok also. Again, it is not your job to convince anyone. Your job is to share your own story. Be true to your story.

2) Listen to others beliefs. If you want to build a relationship with them that is authentic, its important to know what they believe. Yes, even if its different that what you believe. Understanding an individual and listening to their own perspective creates a bridge for open communication. The conversation needs to be two-sided not one-sided to be healthy.

3) Live your beliefs. We all make mistakes but if you say you believe something, please oh please, live by it. This quote sums this concept up perfectly:

Preach the gospel at all times, if necessary use words.
– Saint Francis of Assisi

Q & A for Faith:

Q: My friend always says she wants to pray with me, should I say yes?

A: I am a big believer in the power of prayer. The bible says wherever two or more are gathered in His name, He is with us. This is a promise I love. In general, praying for someone is very harmless. If you don't know what you believe I doubt praying is going to bother you. Generally it's fairly quick and it's a conversation with God. I pray all the time, when driving, brushing my teeth, etc. I think we make it more scary than it needs to be. The more you talk with God through praying, the more comfortable you will be most likely. I think its pretty awesome that your friend wants to pray with you. To me it's the greatest gift we can give each other.

> Pray, and let God worry.
>
> – Martin Luther

Q: I would love my adult children to come with me to church but they never do and it frustrates me, how can I encourage them to come?

A: This is a common wish of parents and while I totally get it, I also understand your adult child's perspective. If you love church, awesome, so glad you've found your faith and are part of a nourishing community. However, I can tell you many individuals who feel forced to attend church have a hard time connecting with a real relationship with God. Just because someone comes to church doesn't mean they are going to be open to hearing or knowing God. I think asking kindly once in a while makes sense since it is a big part of your life but nagging won't do your relationship any good. Praying is my primary piece of advice that they find a church where they can grow in their faith, even if it isn't your church. Their faith will be stronger if it is their own and not piggybacked on yours.

Q: How do you personally interact with individuals who have a lifestyle that isn't inline with your faith?

A: I love that you asked this question. I think many people who have strong faith are judged before they are even given a chance to get to know individuals who may think they are going to be judged or not liked. I personally love people, period. I am not the judge or jury in anyone's story. I make it a goal of mine not to make individuals who are different from I am feel like I am judging them. Instead treating people as people with their whole story is the best way I've found to get to know them. I am thankful for my work that has given me the opportunity to be on teams with all different nationalities and preferences.

Q: What is your stance on abortion, homosexuality, divorce, etc.?

A: This is such a common question and I think it is really the wrong question. I have beliefs on every single one of these and would share them if you wanted me to speak into your story but every circumstance is different and is based in relationship as to whether I would speak my thoughts openly or not. For exercising the purpose of this book, just think of your position on these topics, then imagine I believe the exact opposite of you and see if you can love me in that. I most likely don't believe the exact opposite as you but this is a good exercise to practice the concept of this book. I love this quote, "I don't have a stance, I stand on the word of God," - Shane Holden. This hits home for me because it isn't on my agenda to do anything but love people where they are and with what their experience is. I won't agree with everyone on every topic but I refuse to believe that means we can love one another well regardless.

Q: I do not believe in God. How do you explain the atrocious things that happen in this world if there is a God?

A: I have always felt God in my life from a young age. I have seen Him work miracles and move mountains in my life. I have felt His peace that passes understanding. My faith is synonymous with my experience of who He is. For me that question would be the same as saying you don't believe in my earthly father, they are equally as real to me. As for the atrocities of this world, I don't know fully, I do know sin has a role in it. I do know that it hurts God to see His children hurt.

This poem resinates with me when I think about your question, I have faith that there is victory in the end.

One Little Word

And though this world, with devils filled,
should threaten to undo us,
we will not fear, for God hath willed
his truth to triumph through us.

The Prince of Darkness grim,
we tremble not for him;
his rage we can endure,
for lo, his doom is sure;
one little word shall fell him.

- Martin Luther,
A Mighty Fortress Is Our God

Q: Do you take drugs? Why are you always so happy?

A: Ok, first this made me laugh very hard. I do not take drugs and you can ask either of my children I am not always happy. I do, however, on most days have the joy of the Lord in my heart and it lives in me. I believe that the pain and struggles of this world are nothing compared to the kingdom. I love this quote, it is how I think of God in the midst of our bad days.

The most important lesson that I have learned is to trust God in every circumstance. Lots of times we go through different trials and following God's plan seems like it doesn't make any sense at all. God is always in control and he will never leave us.

– Allyson Felix

Q: How did you come to believe Jesus rose from the dead? I'm still feeling unsure about all the details of the Bible so this is tough for me, meaning I don't fully trust it yet.

A: Interesting question, there is a good book by a scientist called the case for Christ that is worth reading if you want to know more. I believe it because He is real to me, meaning I feel His presence and a peace when I pray to Him. I believe He lives in me and that spirit is alive. I haven't gotten into the archaeological perspective, my experience and general faith leads me there. A bit tough to explain in words actually.

Q: My question is about hell. Do you believe some people go there when they die?

A: Hell, such a tricky one, I do. I haven't read a ton about it and think it gets hard to say who that some is as I see God as the ultimate judge. For instance my loved one was the first one who told me he gave his life to Jesus when I was like 17, he did a lot of gnarly things and some believe took his own life. I don't believe that personally and I actually believe I will see him in heaven because of him telling me of his commitment to God. It is a hope I cherish and can't wait to hug him so tightly. I think this hell concept is very hard for us to fathom, feels so big. I trust God's word though and so I believe Him in that.

TRUTH

**Dear children, let us not love with words or speech
but with actions and in truth.**

– 1 John 3:18

There is one area that I received input on that causes strife when trying to love which really just rubs me wrong. Most areas I can be relaxed and think eternally about but the one that really gets me is gossip. Speaking falsities against each other is something that I just really can't stand. So this chapter in particular is for me, I'm writing to myself about how to love individuals who cause all sorts of damage because they lie, gossip or misconstrue issues by not going to the source.

Whoever is careless with the truth in small matters cannot be trusted with important matters. - Albert Einstein

Careless is such a good word here. If there is one message to this book it is to be careful with our relationships when trying to love those that we have a particularly challenging time loving. Caring about one another looks very different when it comes to truth. It means we don't just lay into someone with our truth. It also means we hold truth and the weight of it in high regard. It means if we have a question about someone, we approach them in love and we ask them, we don't ask their friends about it, we don't ask their kids about it, we ask them. If we can't be bold enough to carefully ask the source something, then we need to forget about it because it must not be important enough to seek truth.

What we don't do is think we know the truth, spread what we think we know, and circle around the source without giving them the respect and care to allow them to own their own story. I think gossipers in particular are story stealers. Loving each other is recognizing that someone's life is their story and honoring them to be brave and bold enough to live it, even if you disagree with it. Story stealers don't love the individual enough to be real and truthful about what's going on. Instead they steal a story by recreating it when they have no right to do so.

A psalm I visit often when I feel under attack by lies is below, it reminds me who I am and whose I am. It reminds me that I do not retaliate and I do not talk bad about others. I am called to love them and speak truth in love.

> The one whose walk is blameless,
> who does what is righteous,
> who speaks the truth from their heart;
> whose tongue utters no slander,
> who does no wrong to a neighbor,
> and casts no slur on others.
>
> Psalm 15:2-3

Tips for Truth:

1) If you didn't hear it from the source, don't believe it and by all means don't pass it on. This is not your story, if you care about the person SO much talk with them, hear them and know the truth. If someone asks you about their story, because you are in a close relationship with them, guard their story and

redirect the inquirer to them. This is how we protect one another from hurt.

2) If your belief system as it relates to truth is different from someone else's, this is ok. Don't be unkind or disrespectful about what they believe. It takes nothing away from your beliefs that someone else believes something different. Tolerance for different views allows for authentic honest relationships.

Q AND A FOR TRUTH:

Q: A friend never admits to doing anything wrong, how can I ever work through to the truth if I don't trust them to tell the truth?

A: Trust is absolutely built on truth. If an individual continually lies to you, its very difficult to have any kind of healthy relationship. I think being bold about saying I feel misled by you because of a history of lies, can we start completely over and I'll forget about the past and believe that you can tell me the truth going forward. If you love this person enough to keep them in your story I think a clean slate, truly without reliving the past is the best way to move forward. If they continue to lie after this do-over, I'd review how strong a role you want this person to have in your story. Without truth, there can't be trust.

Q: My family member always comes to me to act as the mediator between them and another family member? It makes me feel uncomfortable to be in this position but I have done it so long, how do I change it?

A: First, it is wonderful that your family member sees you as a logical fair individual, enough to mediate on their behalf. This relationship sounds like this family member trusts you quite a bit. You are feeling the discomfort of this unhealthy triangle. I would be proactive in this situation and let the family member know that you want to talk with them about something important, try to talk in person. Let them know that you love them and the other family member too much to be in the middle. It isn't your place to act on behalf of another and they really need to just talk directly. If the family member persists that they just can't talk with them, then suggest a professional counselor if they want to work on their relationship. Let the family member know that you want to build a relationship on your own relationship not as a third party. If they honor your request it is a good sign that they respect and love your relationship enough to change it for the better.

6

POLITICS

To err is human. To blame someone else is politics.
– Hubert H. Humphrey

I'll start this chapter by saying I don't even have cable, I also don't subscribe to regular political news updates. However, this topic was one of the hot buttons that cause strife in relationships and loving each other so let's roll.

Since forever, individuals have been looking to humans as idols. They want a savior in a fancy suit who says all the right things and they think will do them as well. This is just unrealistic. My faith informs me that there are no perfect people. The shinier our politicians look the more I wonder what their character consists of. Regardless of which political camp you belong, I can love you just fine even if I don't agree with your politics at all. How do I know this? Because its just flat out true. I choose what I get passionate and angry about. I choose what is just too much to restore a relationship over. I choose when to speak and when not to. I also chose if I am going to value the real relationships that I have as opposed to the false idols who are projected on newspapers and tv screens.

Here is the mystery to me, movie stars remind me a great deal of politicians however family feuds over movie stars are much less frequent even though I'm sure there are equal difference of opinion. The difference here is that we believe politicians have control of our land and destiny. This is one area where my faith helps inform me that no one on this earth has rein over me. Even if a politician decided to take away my rights, and quality of life, I know whose country I belong to. I belong to God's country.

Therefore, I wouldn't say I don't care at all about politics because I do, I just don't care enough about them to wreak havoc on my loved ones and my relationships with them. I would challenge that if you are having major challenges getting along with individuals who have different political views than you, this isn't the only area that you disagree with them. It is most likely just one point of data for many that exist. So the decision is will you allow yourself to get so upset that you cause strife in your relationship or is that relationship too important to you for disrespect. As a peacemaker, engaging in political debates is not something I believe serves a great purpose, unless you are trying to get into office or in a forensics class. Otherwise blasting someone on social media with your justified views, only tears down your relationship and definitely is counter to loving them. If you truly want to have a discussion with them, then schedule time, invite them, have it in person and bring your open ears and heart to listen to them. At the end, you most likely will still disagree but you'll have given the relationship the proper approach and respect.

Tips for Politics:

1) If you want to debate, do it fairly. No online squabbles that escalate, no half-informations, below the belt attacks, or generalizations about a certain party as it relates to an individual.

2) Be informed if you are going to have a strong opinion. Know your facts, if you are going to engage in the type of discussion that you are going to project your opinions do your research.

It reminds me of how people debate about sports teams. The people who have the strongest arguments are the ones who know both, strengths and weaknesses inside and out. They don't just know their team's stats, they research all the information to be informed before they engage in the debate.

3) Walk away. If you truly feel like you are not going to be able to handle yourself in a respectful loving way, walk away. Be authentic with the struggle by explaining that you really value your relationship and its worth more than this disagreement, you can see that you are getting upset so you'd like to respectfully switch topics. Hopefully your loved one will get it, if not, they may need another round of the same calm boundaries expressed that you're not going any further until you can calm down and reengage in love.

Q AND A FOR POLITICS:

Q: My family member de-friends-me before every election, it really bothers me that they are so offended by my opinions that they can't even see them, is this normal?

A: So I definitely am not an expert on normal, I can see how this would hurt your feelings though. I would guess that you two aren't extremely close and there may be other tensions in your relationship. It may actually be a healthy way for them to deal with disagreeing with you and not causing more discord or strife between you two. I think I'd work on the relationship offline, call or visit them and talk about general life. What they did today? If they'd seen any good movies, etc? Focusing on fairly safe topics will help them know that you want a relationship outside of the political tension. If you don't want one though, just let it be and reduce the expectation that they can be the way you want them to be about it.

Q: How can you possibly love someone who agrees with abortion?

A: Easily, their opinions don't change my opinion on a topic. Whether I agree or disagree with them, they are a human who deserves to be listened to, respected and loved. You can put in any major hot topic and the intention is division. My intension is not division, I can respectfully disagree with someone without being mean to them or discrediting who they are as a person.

Q: Aren't politicians all crooks any way, why would anyone choose sides?

A: This is a black and white perspective on a gray area. Just like in any profession there are some politicians who make choices that you disagree with and some who make choices that you agree with. Our political legacy is based on this system, is it flawed? I can't imagine it not being. However, I do believe most politicians enter into the world of politics because they want to make it better. I think it can be a challenging system to change, not impossible but also not the hope I cling to.

> "When I was a boy and I would see scary things in the news, my mother would say to me, Look for the helpers. You will always find people who are helping."
> – Fred Rogers

Whenever I read this quote, I get hopeful. I love the idea of finding the good in a bad situation, the hope this brings. There is also great truth in this quote. People do want to help, many people. This is a beautiful truth, there are also individuals who do not want to help and this is a sad truth. By us looking for the helpers, we are not feeding into the fear that those who want to hurt gain power through. Instead, we are encouraging loving and navigating the gray areas where its hard to see what is always good and always bad.

EXPECTATIONS

Many people feel so pressured by the expectations of others that it causes them to be frustrated, miserable and confused about what they should do. But there is a way to live a simple, joy-filled, peaceful life, and the key is learning how to be led by the Holy Spirit, not the traditions or expectations of man.

– Joyce Meyer

By far the number one reason it seems loving through disagreeing is a challenge, is expectations. This was an interesting finding and took me until the last chapter to assimilate all of the feedback I had received on.

It makes sense though doesn't it, we have certain expectations about every person we interact with. These expectations come from our own beliefs and experiences. Many times they aren't even verbalized which can be the challenge as well. However, verbalized or not, they are their like giant weights around our necks blocking us from truly connecting in an authentic way because my expectations inform what you should do.

Let's take a moment and think about this should word. Should is another story stealing word. It removes an individual's ability to write their own story by imposing expectations on them. Each individual is wired differently, success may look differently to them than you, love may look differently to them than you, they are the ones who live and die with the consequences of what they choose.

I get it, you love them so you want to help them by making sure they don't fall into something bad by placing expectations on them. I would argue that these expectations do nothing but cause a wedge between your relationship with them. My comments relate to adults here, as we all know expecting a child to help with chores is part of building their sense of family and community. However, let's take for a moment an adult with a similar concept. An adult has a very dirty desk at work, so dirty that it seems to be moving. The consequence to this adult's habit is that there documents may be harder to find, they may have leftover food on them, and the adult may come across as unprofessional. These are all natural consequences to a choice the adult is making. Now, let's rewind and apply your projecting expectations on this situation. You tell the adult that you as their coworker expect them to clean their desk, they get frustrated with you and the way you act better than them. They half clean up their desk just so you won't talk with them again about it but there is a wedge now between you and them because they feel judged.

Now this is a minor example however I think it applies to major ones as well. Consequences occur from individuals living their story how they are going to live them. If you are negatively impacted by their choices, that is where boundaries and honest communication come into play but projecting your expectations, should statements, guilt talks will do nothing to strengthening a relationship.

Let's talk for a bit about money because that was a hot topic that I believe falls into this category. The hot topic of money and how individuals spend money, save money, give money, collect money were all served up as causing strife. This is not surprising as we know that for many money is an idol. I would argue that if you are frustrated about what someone else is spending money on, unless it directly impacts you, it's an area to let free. I just don't see it being any different from other parts of someone's story. For instance, if I want to give all my money to a village and live off the land, if this doesn't impact you, you can totally disagree with it, or not understand it but I believe you can still love me. Or let's say that I work three full-time jobs to give my kids every single possession they want and you really value quality time more than material possessions, you can disagree with me and you can also chose whether or not this is going to cause strife and wedge itself in-between our relationship.

Now here's the rub and the part that requires some real heart to hearts as well as care. It's ok for you to communicate that you don't agree with your loved ones, it's not ok to remove your love from them. Loving them regardless of you agreeing or disagreeing is where the beauty in authentic no expectation relationships lie.

I have friends whom this world might call minimal as far as not only their station in life, but their level of intelligence and buying power. These friends to me have been some of the greatest blessings that I've known. - Fred Rogers

This quote hit the mark for me, we can't believe what the world calls success is the only definition and acknowledging that there are many definitions that are different from expectations is where freedom lies and strong relationships thrive.

Tips for Expectations:

1) Don't have them. Instead operate in a place of love, allowing an individual to write their story. If you have the awesome honor of influencing their story, wonderful. Do so with great care and have no expectations in return. Then whatever blessing you receive from the relationship will be a gift instead of an unmet expectation.

2) Discuss what you would like to happen if it's really important to you. This way if you just can't omit the expectation, its known instead of a surprise obstacle that causes guilt and pain.

3) Live in a place of love not of believing you have power of someone. You are the only adult who can change. You can help model and pray for change in others but that's their story to write not yours.

When the power of love overcomes the love of power
the world will know peace.
                                        – Jimi Hendrix

4) Do your best. You are going to fall sometimes but God gives grace for those who have a "want to" love one another. Make sure your heart is in the right place and if you fall once or twice, get right back up and try to help another brother or sister in love.

I tell you the truth, whatever you did for one of the
least of these brothers of mine, you did for me.
                                        – Matthew 25:35-40

Q & A FOR EXPECTATIONS:

Q: My parents want me to do everything the same as them, how do I help them to see that I am a different person?

A: You are on a great start by articulating it exactly this way. I would guess that your parents are operating from a place of fear or expectation. Having a real heart-to-heart about this being your life and you owning the consequences of your choices is a good first start.

Q: I have really high expectations of others and even higher expectations of myself, how do I relax on expecting too much?

A: This takes a lot of practice. The first is to recognize that no one is perfect. The second is to gain some perspective. Researching other countries and realities of other people groups has really helped me in this area. I try to remember that no one is perfect and I let myself off the hook for having to be. I remember grace and that if I am trying my best, that is really all I can do. I try very hard not to expect things of others and if I have expectations that I just can't let free, I communicate why they are important to me to the appropriate person and then let them free. I try to remember that grace has been given to me and I have the awesome choice to give it to others, unmerited favor, what a gift and a blessing.

PART

2

LEADING WELL, NAVIGATING
THE GRAY AT WORK

You are the leader of your career, behaviors, attitude,
words, actions and choices.

FEEDBACK

Feedback is the breakfast of champions.
– Ken Blanchard

Feedback: for most of us, this gift isn't our first choice to receive. The term, whether we call it feedback, input, constructive criticism, or collaboration, resonates with most of us as a negative instead of positive. I soundly think that an individual's ability to appropriately respond to and incorporate feedback makes or breaks leaders.

There are two sides to the "feedback gifting" equation: giving and receiving. In today's workplace, the ability to refine both skills is critical to leading well. Feedback is an art-form. Most people would prefer to opt out of participating because frankly, it takes some serious effort to articulate feedback in a constructive way. It is even more challenging to receive it in a wise way.

Below are my top 3 tips for both giving and receiving feedback in a way that promotes leading well.

How to Effectively Give Feedback

> Be selective. Make sure it's observed as a trend, because everyone has a bad day once. Ensure the

feedback is based on a pattern that is causing the individual to reach an outcome that is not the desired one. Ensure the feedback is important enough to make a difference, as opposed to coming across as "nitpicking." Plan appropriately to ensure sharing this feedback is actually helpful.

Be gentle. Receiving input that has to do with changing behavior is not easy. Recognize this and think about how to express the input gently. Each recipient has a different tolerance for directness with coaching. Ideally, you'll know your team member well enough to determine the best approach. With that said, always err on the side of being as gentle as possible during the feedback phase. If the behavior escalates to the point where it requires advanced coaching or disciplinary action, that is a different story. But for simple feedback, gentle is better.

Be encouraging. Once you've shared the primary feedback, prepare to share a couple positives from the situation. Provide encouraging observations to relay that your intentions are genuinely intended to support the team member's overall success.

How to Effectively Receive Feedback

Be attentive. Listen carefully and take notes if needed. Be 100% present in this moment to truly hear everything the giver is saying. Resist the urge to let your mind wander to a defensive place or tune the person out. The information they are sharing with you is a gift, and you can choose how to use it.

Be engaged. Restate the feedback and the impact that it is causing, as you have heard it. Make sure this comes across as clarifying the feedback, not discounting it. Ask for ideas and suggestions to handle the particular situation or behavior in a way that would be more beneficial to all involved.

Be appreciative. A team member bringing feedback to you, whether it be your boss, customer, or peer, is a way of them telling you, "I care about your success." Thank them sincerely for the feedback. Let them know that any time they have feedback for you, it is welcomed. This will reinforce the culture of transparency and trust.

Real trust is built on honest dialogue. Receiving and giving feedback is part of honest dialogue. Spending the time, seeing it as a gift, and wrapping it well (whether giving or receiving), will have high returns in your ability to lead effectively. The best teammates are the ones who can be candid with one another. In order to trust each other, highlighting both negative and positive feedback is critical.

Q & A Section for Feedback:

Q: What should I do if I don't agree with the feedback provided?

A: This is the beauty of your life, attitude, words and behavior being your own. You can pleasantly thank someone for their perspective and make the choice to not own that feedback. You get to choose to adopt any feedback that you do agree with and not incorporate any that you don't. Receiving the feedback is the key, receiving it with grace and honestly self-reflecting to see if there is some truth to it. The decision to change is yours though, regardless of others input.

Q: At my company, I get in trouble for telling the truth, honestly how do I provide feedback when they don't want to hear what is really going on?

A: If I had to reduce the responsibilities of a good follower to a single rule, it would be to speak truth to power.— Warren Bennis

This quote comes to mind and when you do try to and it isn't received. This is such a frustrating one. The way I heard this explained once from an employee is that the company actions were so loud, the employee couldn't hear what the company was saying about wanting feedback. I myself think you have to continue speaking truth, I think it can be blanketed in holding the company accountable by asking if they really want to know what you think about a topic or if they just want a head-nod. If they say they do want to know then being extra cautious of your professionalism and tone will be helpful. However, if you find that continually they say they want it and then backlash when you give it, may be time to move on to a company that means what they say.

Q: I feel like my coworkers do not listen to feedback at meetings at all, they come into a meeting already knowing what they are going to say and don't listen, how can my feedback be better heard?

A: Meetings are such a hot button. I always think knowing the type of meeting and purpose for the meeting is key. Also, question is a meeting needed for this type of project/input. They may actually be more receptive to a phone call where you ask if it's ok to share your opinion and then allow them to move forward with that input as they would like to. My take on this is if they don't actually listen, they are the ones losing and really the entire company. We have a group of diverse team members to help ensure we are coming to the best possible outcome. If we short-change any team member's feedback, we are shortchanging the value they bring. I think asking specifically in a meeting, Is this a good time to provide feedback?

Will help set the stage that you would like the mic. Then modeling how you want to be listened to by listening well to others is really all that's directly in your control. If the rejection of feedback is continual with one specific team member at meetings, I'd recommend speaking professional to them about it and giving them a chance to respond/change, they may not even be aware of their tendency to cut you off/reject your feedback.

CHANGE

It is not the strongest or the most intelligent who will survive but those who can best manage change.
– Charles Darwin

Lean principles are key to any successful business. We know this intrinsically, but quantifying and procreating it is a more difficult exercise. I recently toured a completely organic and biodynamic farm. It struck me how incredibly good they are at this topic of continuous improvement. And this is for one key reason—their very survival depends on it.

For example, it takes several years to even qualify as an organic farm. This means that similar to the journey many companies are on to permeate the lean culture throughout every level of their organization (refining who you're going to be, how you're going to be it, and obtaining any type of title associated with those efforts), the endeavor is a marathon...not a sprint.

Another example is the term biodynamic, which in the sense of farming, observes treating the entire farm as one ecosystem. They must understand how one influence (pigs for instance) impacts and affects another (apple orchard soil). This enterprise-wide view is key to continuous improvement, because a company is a living breathing organism where every part affects another.

The tour hit home when the farmer explained they had to tear out an entire section of a particular crop variety because it didn't work well with the farm's overall objective. The cost of maintaining it would have been simply too high, taking the entire farm into account. This bold decision to conserve the main goal, even if it caused a temporary loss, was inspiring. The practice of lining up products, work, and resources to really see how they are benefiting the primary goal, and then having the courage to take a loss in order to focus on the greater good, is an exercise every great leader should utilize more often.

My final observation from this tour, and how it relates to our business world, is one of continuous experimentation. This goes hand in hand with continuous improvement. The rigor with which they tried new things continually struck me. There was a growing tunnel built purely for experimentation, and it was used to test new ways of doing things...and often, those experiments failed! However, sometimes a success turned into the next big thing that led to another season of earnings. This commitment to innovation is a big one. The time, energy, and resources involved in testing something every single day of the year is a discipline that many companies could learn from.

Following is some key continuous improvement takeaways from farming that also apply in the conference room:

> Don't be hasty. Behavioral, and cultural change in particular, takes time. Make sure you are planning and investing in the long haul. For any real change in problem solving and innovation to stick, it needs to have deep roots throughout all levels of the organization.

One world. Although your efforts with continuous improvement may be departmental, you're measuring of it needs to be company-wide. Thinking of behavioral or cultural change in silos works best with coaching and specific corrective focus, but it shouldn't be used as the example for how to measure your total company's progress. Lean toward thinking of the progress report as the slowest adopter. Once that group is making progress, you'll see the ripple effects increase. The term tilth in farming comes to mind. Tilth is used to describe "the general health of the soil including a balance of nutrients, water, and air. Soil that is healthy and has good physical qualities is in good tilth."

Be a bold pruner. If one crop, product line, resource, and so on, is causing a detrimental outcome for the whole farm, its time to take the short-term loss and invest in the long-run. This takes far more courage than we often realize.

Try something new everyday. We can't be certain what the next high yield or greater efficiency is. Therefore, we need to continually be on the lookout, investing in testing strategies, asking questions, and trying new techniques. In the interest of leading well, be sure you are as diligent at learning from your failures as reveling in your successes. There is great benefit to both.

Q & A Section for Change:

Q: My company talks about change but I just think they mean more work for me or being laid off, how can I trust that change is good?

A: Companies have different levels of transparency with change. The best are highly upfront and honest about what the business reasons are for change. However, some are not. Change is just change, not necessarily good or bad. However, your ability to respond to change is directly in your control. Your attitude towards the change, communication about how business is impacted by the change, what change may be needed based on this initial change. These are all ways to ensure you are leading yourself well through change. I have learned throughout my career to find the opportunity in the change and to lead change. Change itself is just change, how we influence and respond to it makes all the difference.

Q: I'm thinking about what type of work I want to do and how to develop myself, what are your suggestions?

A: I love this topic! Developing yourself and your credentials is totally in your control. You can't control the bosses you will have necessarily or the changes that are done to you. However, you can control the changes you make in your career and your own development. As a team member, I encourage you to imbed the continuous improvement mentality into your every day. Know where you need to be and what it will take to get there. Also, make sure the type of work you take on brings you great happiness. You can have joy no matter what through the spirit but having work that is meaningful to you will make for a happier life. You'll be able to motivate yourself by tangibly feeling the value you are bringing.

Q: My company seems to change things that don't need to be changed and not change areas that really need to change? Why does this happen?

A: There could be a couple reasons for this. The first is the company may be disconnected from the actual work and therefore not understand impacts of changes imposed. A second, more common one is that they haven't highlighted the true change reason to a large population, this causes doubt where there shouldn't be doubt. For instance, if there are great economic savings by making a change, share this information. By sharing it, the employees understand that the business is taking prudent measures to ensure they are acting fiscally responsible, not just arbitrarily making changes. The second half of your question is about change that needs to happen, make sure you are doing your best to be empowered and make this change happen. Talk with who you need to, document what you need to and be part of the solution not the problem with communicating needed change.

HOPE

There was never a night or a problem that could defeat sunrise or hope.

– Bernard Williams

When I think of the greatest leaders, there are many characteristics that come to mind, like integrity, grit, intelligence, and creativity. The one that has resonated more recently with me is hope. I'm not talking about a flighty, unfounded hope. I am talking about a well-reinforced hope in seeing the opportunities that might not be readily visible in a given situation.

A leader is an individual who sees a business, product, or team member and identifies how it can be better than it is. They then cast this vision, remove obstacles, and support their team on the path to success along the way. At its core, this process is hope in action. A leader uses hope as a verb, defined as "looking forward to with desire and reasonable confidence" or "to believe, desire, or trust." Hope is necessary for a leader to invoke change. If they don't have the seedling of hope, they won't see the possibilities and move toward the actions of turning them into a reality.

A leader who I respect once asked a colleague, "Are you hoping or knowing?" The best leaders do both. They start with a hope of a possible disrupter or change, and they gain confidence in their ability to know it can work. Then they influence others to become advocates for it and create a contagious hope that turns into sweat, smarts, and work.

I pondered why hope isn't one of the foundational leadership terms we frequently use, and I came to a conclusion: we are not comfortable with possibly being wrong. But great leaders have to be comfortable risking that they may be wrong, and wise enough to know when they are. This requires another H word: humility. I would challenge that as leaders, we must be comfortable with words like hope, dream, and believe being a core part of who we are. If we don't allow ourselves to hope, dream, and believe, how can we expect our teams to?

Following is some key hope takeaways:

> Optimism is just as contagious as pessimism. Being an optimistic leader doesn't mean you aren't going to hold individuals accountable. It means you are positive about the company and its future. If you want to impact your team's attitude, try optimism.

> Being hopeful does not mean you don't need to put in the work. Success takes work, smarts, and sweat. A positive outlook and ability to see an opportunity doesn't lighten in any way the amount of real hard work that needs to accompany hope. Hope is the positive confidence that helps steer and influence the "validation then confirmation" work.

> Dream big. Our ability to be hopeful allows us to dream, which allows us to create in a unique way. We see a problem or opportunity differently when we allow ourselves the time and freedom to dream big. The future workplace will have plenty of opportunities

for creative leaders who dream big, hope fruitfully, and implement creative solutions. Be one of those kind of leaders.

Q & A Section for Hope:

Q: Hope is such a fluffy word, what place does it really have in a professional environment?

A: Hope as a word is just like any other one. It's the way we take action with these types of words, Hope/Integrity/Ethics that makes the difference in a work place. Having empty hope is absolutely fluffy and does not belong in the work place. However, having a vision for a solution to a problem, a new way of thinking, an optimism for change absolutely belong in the work place, hope in a pragmatic actionable form is essential.

Q: I work with people who put down my beliefs and even say my God's name in vain regularly, how can I have hope in such a discouraging atmosphere?

A: Oh this question just makes me want to give you a hug first of all. It can be hard on our spirits to hear others put down the very beliefs that help us wake up in the morning. The first thing to think about is most likely, they are not doing this to cause you to be uncomfortable, it is most likely just how they live. Although different from your way of talking or living, it is their right to speak within reason in a way that is different from yours. However, if they are actually bullying you with this, I think a firm bold stand of directly saying, I'm sure you don't mean anything by it (giving benefit of doubt no matter what) but it would really mean a lot to me and my work experience if you didn't say X or Y. They may not ever change but you will have brought to light something that has been bothering you and in that, if done respectfully, you'll feel better. If you choose to have this hard conversation, I recommend praying a ton before and after. You'll want a calm, presence of kindness to be the tone of the conversation regardless of what it is met with by the receiver.

COACHING

Each person holds so much power within themselves that needs to be let out. Sometimes they just need a little nudge, a little direction, a little support, a little coaching, and the greatest things can happen.
– Pete Carroll

I recently attended a global leadership event where Marcus Buckingham made this bold statement: "If you don't want to be a coach, don't be a leader."

His words resonated deep into the core of what I have found to be the key component to building great teams. Conversely, coaching is also the missing ingredient in leaders who don't make an impact. Great leaders know how and when to roll up their sleeves and work right next to their teammates. Coaching alongside during the practices, injuries, and personal and professional trials is what binds trust between the coach, player, and team.

Being a coach differs in a monumental way from just being the boss. It is the inherent investment that is implied. A coach is invested in the player and knows what each player needs to do to make the team the best team it can be. A coach knows the strengths and weaknesses of each individual on the team. A coach handles this information with extreme care, which I would argue is critical for building trust.

There are definitely times when disciplinary action is necessary, but I would challenge that the large majority of situations could start with good-intentioned coaching, where an employee feels invested in. When an employee feel invested in, everyone wins. The company wins because the employee is engaged and contributing at a high value. The boss wins because the relationship with the employee isn't strained; it is honest, collaborative, and based on working through issues instead of avoiding them. The employee wins because she knows where she is at as far as performance is concerned; she has had the chance to make mistakes, learn from them, and move forward as a team.

Following is some key coaching takeaways:

> Don't be a leader if you're not willing to coach. Coaching takes time, energy, effort, learning, and purposeful practice. If you aren't going to commit to coaching, don't be a leader.

> Sweat currency—spend time doing the hard work. The last way to earn the respect of your team is by taking the easy work. Instead, take on one of the more challenging projects and work it with them as a team. This shows that you are willing to put in the effort just like you are asking the team to. This resembles when a coach runs alongside the team or does push-ups with them. Show them you can still put in the sweat currency.

> Learn from the team. The beauty of the coach–team relationship is that the learning goes both ways. Team members can help teach a coach the way to

get their best work. Watch for these moments when your employees show you how to lead them through various coaching methods.

Q and A for Coaching:

Q: I barely have time to get my work done, how do I make time to coach on top of that? Also, shouldn't they have gotten all the coaching before they got to this level?

A: I would argue that if you don't make the time to coach, your team isn't operating at its full potential and you aren't leading. There are rewards of coaching but they are not immediate, it generally takes more time before it takes less. The relationship grows, trust grows, there are minor observations of change if fostered over time become long-standing improvements. Coaching is the work of the best leaders because it is serving for the entire organizations health, productivity and overall good, not just an immediate check mark on a list. I'd recommend reassessing what you consider, your work, and including coaching in there with your leadership standard work.

Q: My direct report wanted to give me a coachable moment, isn't this disrespectful?

A: First, thank you for asking this very direct question. Coachable moments are not confined from you to your direct reports but multi-directional. Coachable moments, a moment when someone shares something about their perception of you, is to be valued. As long as their tone and overall approach is respectful welcome this opportunity to receive their input with open ears. Your response will help set the tone for how they too receive your coachable moments.

GRIND/BURN-OUT

Leadership is an active role; 'lead' is a verb. But the leader who tries to do it all is headed for burnout, and in a powerful hurry.

– Bill Owens

I often hear professionals talk about the grind of their work. This word, "Grind" is sometimes replaced with burn-out or busyness. Even more professionals seem to be ground or burned out already when they are sharing about their workloads.

This approach of being in the grind, then ground is one that I spent my first ten years living. There was always something that needed to keep me late, work longer hours, the weekend, through my vacation, etc. In truth, there were two factors at play. The first was my inability to set realistic boundaries about deadlines and workload. The second was half my experience prioritizing my time, and half my ability to truly depend on a team. There are some excellent lessons that come from being in this place and living through it, however it cannot be maintained over the long-term. Leading well is about knowing yourself, being aware of when you need to step-up to get something done and when you aren't the right person to make it happen and getting out of their way. Communication is key to managing your career, whether navigating the grind, getting un-ground or gaming-on.

Below are my top 3 tips for navigating the Grind:

> Be Specific: If there is a task, project, work in general that needs to be done, be specific about what is expected. Work, rework and additional work is inefficient and too often a symptom of the Grind. This doesn't mean that you won't need to be flexible if outcome demands change but you'll have a bit more leverage because expectations were specific at the onset.

> Be Self-Aware: People have different skills and let's be honest, work is accomplished better and faster when those skills are honed. If you are not the best skilled for a specific task, communicate this. Communicate it in a way that expresses that you will be glad to spend the time learning from someone who has the skill, or through self-study but acknowledge that it may not be the most efficient way to get from A to Z.

> Keep your perspective: I have yet to take a vacation, when it was the ideal time. The truth is if you are adding value to your company and thriving in a career, there will never be a great time to take time for you. Navigating the grind is knowing that there will always be something that pops-up and sometimes you need to handle it, sometimes you need to trust your team and coach upon your return, sometimes you need to just let it lie.

Below are my top 3 tips for how to get un-Ground:

> Be Real: Part of being real is acknowledging that you are not performing at your best because the grind has gotten the better of you and you are ground. If

you realize you are ground, that is a better place than not knowing, but it still is going to take some work to fix. Most people aren't even aware that they are ground until they lose it, it could be their job, their temper, their family, their project, etc. There are a lot of indicators that can wake people up. Make sure you are being real with how you are managing the work and don't kid anyone, especially yourself.

Disclose: Talk directly with your supervisor and express that you aren't in a good place as far as workload goes. They may not be receptive, be able to change it, or believe it but this first conversation is critical for getting unground. Until you disclose that the situation is out of hand, it is only going to get worse.

Be part of the solution: Creatively come-up with a couple ways to help make deadlines more realistic, share tasks, provide back-up scenarios. Healthy communication and culture takes both the employee and employer doing their part to solve the root problem. I'd recommend spending some time to really brainstorm how you are getting in your own way in this area. I have seen individuals who are so concerned about their turf that they bury themselves work-wise. Team work will beat I work, 10 times out of 10.

Also, top 3 tips to Game-on:

Do the hard work first: There are activities that we like to do less than other activities but frankly they need to get done. I've found that doing the hard work first, having the tough conversation first, etc., frees up my day to handle the tasks I enjoy a bit more. To game-on and thrive, you need to manage your workload effectively, leading your day well.

Communicate: I can't overemphasize your need to talk with team members, supervisors and direct reports about what you are working on, struggling with, etc. Gaming on effectively means working as a team and it's difficult for people to work as a team when they don't know what is happening in your world. Quick clarification, this isn't a whining or vent session, it is providing an update. Make sure it is relevant, thorough and brief based on the listener. Also, make sure there is an ask for their perspective instead of a monologue by you.

Motivate yourself: Regardless of if you have a hundred direct reports or zero, you are a leader. You lead your work, your attitude, your participation, your part in the culture of work you are part of. It is your job to motivate yourself to navigate the grind well, avoid being ground-up, and gaming on. Your leadership team, HR partners can help guide you, but at the end of the day you know best the effort you are capable of and are responsible to deliver.

Q and A for the Grind/Burn-out:

Q: I want to continue climbing the corporate ladder, how can I possibly say no to an assignment?

A: I suppose my first question would be at what cost are you wanting to climb the corporate ladder and what's at stake? For instance, if you achieve a great promotion but have a deficit of time with your family and loved ones, is this ok with you. If it is, for how long? Is it ok with them? The point actually isn't saying no to the assignment if you are really excited about it, the question is how do you set expectation to succeed with that project and still maintain non-work healthy relationships.

Q: I just don't have enough time to get everything done? What are your suggestions for making more time?

A: This is another challenge moment, I actually think you have more time than you think. How long did you watch tv, shoot the breeze with a friend, sleep, etc.? Now you may want to do all of those things so then the point is to recalibrate what else you can achieve. You may need to say no to somethings because you choose to do other things. Time is not the problem here, expectations and alignment of your activities with desired outcomes is the misalignment to correct.

Q: How do I plan to take vacation when I am buried after even one day off?

A: First of all, planning is the key word. Ensuring that your team knows you'll be unavailable well in advance, that you have avoided any key deadline time frames sets up the team for the best possible success. That said, there is never a good time to take vacation when you are in a fast-moving role. Prepare well and then just turn the electronics off, check email once a day at night if it will make you rest better but don't skip your vacations altogether. You can never get time or your health back. You can always make more money.

FOLLOWING

There are two ways of spreading light: to be the candle or the mirror that reflects it.
– Edith Wharton

Unless you own your business and work completely by yourself, follower-ship is a critical leadership skill. Yes, I said follower-ship is a leadership skill.

Knowing how and when to follow is as important as knowing how and when to lead. I might argue its even more important in certain situations. The way you present yourself on teams speaks volumes about how you expect teams to react to your leadership.

The challenge with follower-ship, as compared to leadership, is that it isn't recognized as critical in the business world. But it is every bit as important as leadership. Being an effective follower is as essential to a plan's success as any other factor. Let's break this down a bit further. As a leader in an organization, your involvement as a lead in different initiatives ebbs and flows. You aren't always the person who is calling the shots. In fact, if your organization is healthy, there will be a high level of collaboration involved up, down, and across the managerial line. Sometimes you wear the hat of a leader, and sometimes the follower hat is the right one to wear. It is of very high importance, and you need to be highly tuned into it.

When trying to advocate for follower-ship in corporate leadership, there's a major obstacle to overcome: credit. If a project goes particularly well, the leader of the project is usually the primary recipient of the credit for success. For a natural leader who has become attached to credit as a form of validation, it can be difficult to participate in a project without receiving the credit for their participation, whether they admit it or not. If you find yourself in this mindset, here's how you overcome it. Move on and be confident in yourself enough to know that you, as a follower, on whichever project was successful, played a key role in that success. The role you played was clarifying questions, supporting the leader's and team's success, keeping to the vision, following direction, and holding yourself and others accountable.We know in today's world, particularly in large organizations, it takes a strong team to achieve success. This is true regardless of how strong a leader is. To quote a colleague, "Its teamwork that makes the dream work."

Now that we dealt with that challenge, let's look at some of the realities of working in a mid-to large-size company. You have a boss, that boss has a boss, and so on. Regardless of how many credentials, letters, and degrees are at the end of your title, even you have a responsibility to be a follower. This is something to be proud of, excel at, and develop every single day.

Follower-ship is a concept that doesn't get as much airplay as leadership. For every 9 people on a 10-person team, there is 1 identified as a leader. That 1 person is no more important than the other 9. They just have a different role. We, as leaders, need to lift up the role of follower and see it for the gem that it is. Following well begets to success as much as leading well does.

I'd like to address another key challenge: you may not agree with your boss, or your boss's boss. As long as it isn't an ethical issue, and you've had your time to present your argument, there is a time to take pride in your ability to carry out an order...an order that you may not fully agree with. Knowing your role in a particular phase and honing this understanding over time is an essential development practice.

Being true to your leadership self involves being an exceptional follower. Don't short change yourself or your team by missing this fact. We can accomplish so much more when we think less about who gets the credit. Instead, put that energy into what success looks like and how to get there together as a team.

Below are some key follower-ship takeaways:

> Follower-ship is critically important. As a leader, it's important that you carry the follower-ship torch, especially when you are seen as a leader in the organization. Make sure that you are recognizing the whole team when you are in a leadership position and supporting with 100% engagement in a follower-ship position.

> Team's win together and lose together. Your participation as a team player is fundamental. Again, unless you work only with and for yourself, you are going to be in various roles throughout your career. Your reputation as a follower or solid team player is trusted and is going to influence your success in the projects you lead more than any other factor.

> Courageous integrity is required. Being good at follower-ship takes courage. It takes being real and honest about concerns and channeling concerns appropriately in a respectful, productive dialogue.

Finally you must put them to rest, trusting and moving on. This engagement requires a high level of courageous integrity.

Q AND A FOR FOLLOWING:

Q: What if I completely disagree with the direction of my boss?

A: This will most likely occur if you have worked together for any period of time. Ask yourself two questions, 1-Is my boss's stance unethical causing me to compromise the business's mission, if the answer is no then ask question 2 - Have I communicated effectively my thoughts and opinions on this topic respectfully with my boss, if the answer is yes to question 2 and no to question 1, then proceed on with executing on your boss's decision or move to a different role/ company.

Q: I way prefer to lead not to follow, what does this say about me?

A: You are most likely just a natural leader, that is awesome! However, there is a time and a place for both. I think just asking yourself should I be the leader in this project/moment or is this a good time to exercise my follower-ship skills is a good first start to moving towards heightened awareness.

Q: Are followers less successful than leaders?

A: Such a great question that strikes that question about the world's definition of success again. I would say they are actually equally successful to the degree that they are executing on the business objective. They are dependent on one another in all ways for the business's success. Once you disconnect one from the other, the team is not working at the full potential.

ACCOUNTABILITY

The best kind of accountability on a team is peer-to-peer. Peer pressure is more efficient and effective than going to the leader, anonymously complaining, and having them stop what they are doing to intervene.

– Patrick Lencioni

Accountability is such an interesting leadership word. I have found that most people who hold themselves accountable are hypersensitive to ensuring they are accomplishing their part. While individuals who struggle with accountability, don't think they are the problem because they just aren't tuned in and may have never been allowed to fail. Yes, I said the word Fail. Most of us will admit that we have learned way more from failure than success. Those lessons have been visceral and fast learning in action.

There is nothing like forgetting your lunch at home and going hungry to remind you to pack it in your bag the next day. When a professor has called us on an assignment that we didn't give our all and we both know it. If a project gets behind and our group is the trailing factor, that pit in our stomach. That feeling of what could we have done to prevent this with all eyes on you. Some of us know that feeling and try to prevent it proactively, others haven't actually gotten to an honest place with the consequences of not being accountable. Sometimes they only way they are being held accountable is when the trend is well work and they are experiencing very dramatic changes made to them not by them.

I remember the first time I had direct reports, I was determined to ensure they were successful. I didn't want them ever to fail at all. The problem is pretty soon there were two of us doing the same job. They were doing it once and I was double taking care of it to ensure we were covered. This was not holding these team members accountable. Now, I know that allowing our team members to be set-up for success but then fail if they do not hold themselves accountability is part of the development process.

They won't always have a supervisor or leader that will set them up for success and they need to define clear expectations early on in their career to ensure they are hitting the mark.

Following are some key accountability takeaways:

> Know what success looks like. Defining expectations is everyone's job, people say. I will tell you, as an individual you want to clearly know what you are on the hook for and which part the team is expecting from you. I would challenge, if you don't know, who does.

> Hold others accountable, kindly. I believe the best in people. This means that I believe people genuinely want to succeed and be a good team player. Developing phrasing that is a kind way of saying, "I felt it was your part to do X, did I miss something?" and a dozen other phrases like this help to kindly clarify what could be a blind spot in process and communication. I also want to take this moment and say what is

non-negotiable. Don't gossip about who doesn't get their work done. This is a complete waste of energy and culturally damaging. If you have repeated gone to an individual in earnest kindness and the pattern continues, escalate to their supervisor in an effort to help, not negatively impact this employee.

Sometimes the answer is no. Part of being accountable is knowing what is and is not achievable. Sometimes the answer needs to be no to unrealistic expectations. It should also be, "I don't see that being able to be accomplished in X days, however we could accomplish it in that time frame with an additional X resources or in X days without those resources". Your integrity with a yes is at stake. We all know things happen and we sometimes need to reset expectation but if you know in your heart it's unrealistic, the best time to correct the expectation is immediately upon receipt of the assignment.

Q and A for Accountability:

Q: How do you hold someone accountable for being lazy at work?

A: Oh how I feel for you with this question. It can be very frustrating when you are holding your own and completing your work on time only to look over and see a coworker wasting away the day. My first suggestion is always to identify the trend with benefit of doubt. Once you see that this trend is occurring regularly, take the issue to the source. Pray about how to convey your frustrating and then say kindly, I feel frustrated because I have a ton to do and it seems like you don't, what am I missing? It may be challenging to be frank and fearless for this topic but its way better than talking about the person behind their back or running to your supervisor to tattle. Particularly if you haven't talked with them before. If you have talked with them several times then bringing a supervisor in may be needed.

Q: What do you do when you realize you have dropped the ball?

A: Be honest and upfront, apologize. Do not create excuses, take complete ownership and allow individuals who are impacted to ask as many questions as they need to. Be honest, forthright and apologetic. Don't hang your head any lower than it needs to hang though, everyone makes mistakes. Recognize though that others may need more time to get over it than you do, be respectful of this!

Q: How do I hold my boss accountable without making them angry?

A: Managing up in a respectful way is one of the most challenging skills to learn. As you well know, the majority of people leave their boss not their company. I believe in honest dialogue about your frustration once you've seen a trend. If your boss is open to self-reflection, they may not like you bringing it up but should respect it.

8

GOSSIP

Be Impeccable With Your Word. Speak with integrity. Say only what you mean. Avoid using the word to speak against yourself or to gossip about others. Use the power of your word in the direction of truth and love.

– Don Miguel Ruiz

Let's talk about the damage that gossip can do and how you can prevent it with direct communication. Gossip is sneaky, it creeps in like a toxin would and undermines transparency and teamwork. The thing is at first it seems like just bonding, or sharing your feelings about another. This is the thing though, as a work environment unless you are a professional counselor or talent assessor, your job most like is not talking about someone else. Your work in general, if you need to talk about an individual, is best directed in a healthy way to that person. Start with the benefit of the doubt. Start with owning what is going on and then communicate in a professional way in a conducive environment what your opinion is.

It takes more courage than most conversations, however, it will build you into a leader who is respected and sleeps well at night. Gossip is like a toxin because you don't necessarily know it is killing your team, it sneaks in and seems harmless at first, then you begin to see the results. There are sideways glances, long conversations with individuals who don't include the actual person who needs to hear the feedback. These all sum up to one word, inefficiency. The most efficient way to have someone know what my opinion is of them or a way that they could improve or were perceived is, drum roll, to tell them. Not to tell the person who I like better, or who always agrees with me but to tell them.

Now let's say you have talked with them about a particular issue and nothing changes, its fine to tell them you're going to need to escalate it. However, my guess is most people don't confront the conversation head-on, instead they go around and around. They talk with who they are comfortable with talking to, most times not the person and nothing changes, except more alienation, less understanding and less productivity.

Following are some key direct communication takeaways:

Don't assume the worst. Instead of believing this particular person knew how the decision they made would impact you negatively, talk with them.

Believe the best, that it was a misunderstanding and they didn't mean to hurt you by saying X. This positioning will help foster a positive work conversation.

Don't gossip. Do not talk about another person, in a negative way. If you have something to say to someone, tell them and only them as frequently as you can. If you must escalate, do. Be respectful, direct and open to their perspective.

Own your behavior. If you make a mistake and catch yourself gossiping, stop. Whether you are at work, at a work related dinner, out and about. Be aware of your own behavior and own it. Stop immediate, say something like, "This actually isn't helpful, I need to just talk with X directly" or redirect the conversation then if it matters to you do talk with the person directly and be done with gossip, it's a toxin for teams, trust me.

Tip for Gossip:

1) If someone is gossiping to you or putting someone down, stop them. There are plenty of kind ways of doing this, you can redirect the conversation. You can ask if they wouldn't talk about that particular person or situation as you'd prefer to talk about something else. You can be completely silent and not feed into the negative putting others down. Nothing good comes from gossip, it tears a part trust and breaks relationships. Act with integrity in all you do and share.

Printed in the United States
By Bookmasters